FOREVER GIRL

FOREVER GIRL

IF YOU FIND HER
KEEP HER

By Kira

Instagram: Kirapoems
Email: xkira111x@hotmail.com

PODCAST

You can also find Kira reading poetry on his podcast
"Forever Girl".
Now available on Apple, Spotify and Google.

♛ ♦ ♀ ✦ ♥ 🍓 ♠ ☾

DEDICATION

A love letter
dedicated to my one and only forever girl.

♛ ♦ ♀ ✦ ♥ ♥ ♠ ☾

CONTENTS

FOREVER GIRL

i called her my forever girl
because it's only with her
i felt the need
for a never-ending
romance

♛ ♦ ♀ ✦ ♥ 🦋 ♠ ☾

all i need
is a little bit of moonlight
a drop of wine
and you

girls like you
are what homes
are made of

♛   ♦   ♀   ✦   ♥   ❦   ♠   ☾

she believed her scars
to be an ugly truth
but still to this day
i see them
as a beautiful blueprint
of the journey
that created my world

to love is beautiful
to be loved is special
but to love and be loved
by the one you love
is a miracle
only a few can say
they have known

i swear to you
she would sparkle in the night
and i would sleep
in awe
of the magic
that lay beside me

how long do you wait
to band the fingers of fate in metal
how long do you wait
to place diamond between knuckles
there will never be a perfect time
to say i love you dearly
so why not do it now
while there's still stars in our eyes

♛　♦　♀　✦　♥　☽　♠　☾

you should see her
in moonlight

i guarantee
she'll have your heart on one knee
promising her the stars

her love's for sale
it costs one true heart
and a lifetime of kisses

♛ ♦ ♀ ✦ ♥ ☙ ♠ ☾

he promised
to place the universe
inside her hand
and with that
she held his heart
and whispered
"it already is"

i wanted to be
the wind beneath her wings
because angels like her
deserve to be up high
soaring above the clouds
on show for the galaxy to see

we gazed out
at the beautiful twilight
kissed by starlight
moon-soaked
and mesmerised

i keep having this dream of us
two star-crossed lovers
playing like children in the snow
writing love poems
on the frosted canvas beneath our feet
and we would sip wine
with eyes sweeping along the timberline
this silly dream of mine
outside our log cabin
in a swedish forest
two lovers in heaven

love is a kiss
that's caught fire

we counted stars under the moonlight
but every time we did
she always forgot to count herself
then i would remind her
and she would reply
"i'm not a star silly boy"
at which point
i would look at her in confusion
because she would shine just like one

♛ ♦ ♀ ✦ ♥ 🐨 ♠ ☽

i believe in god
simply because
you can't be randomness
formed into perfection

you are eternally ashamed
of being who you are
why do you concern yourself
with the opinions of others?
a queen of beauty
a piece of heaven
still you hate yourself more and more
deep inside i know emptiness weighs the most
and every thought is a battle
but they will never understand a girl so rare
you are a diamond in the hands
of devils

i wasn't afraid to die
i was afraid to live
you gave me a reason
to stay

i'm just a boy in my room
writing poems
about the girl of my dreams
hoping to one day
make her my wife

when she laughs
everything else in my world disappears
all that's left
is us
just two perfect people
inside a perfect moment
in perfect love

♛ ♦ ♀ ✦ ♥ ☙ ♠ ☾

she looks at me like a da vinci painting
perfect in every way
she listens to me like a symphony
composed by mozart
she touches me like i am gold
so valuable and irreplaceable
she loves me like royalty
and i love her the same

♛ ♦ ♀ ✦ ♥ 🐣 ♠ ☾

you sit there
with your dandelions
thinking, thinking

your head's
a beautiful mess

she was a magician in the way
she could hide her bad days
smiling, smiling, smiling
you'd never know
you never did know

♛ ♦ ♀ ✦ ♥ 🍂 ♠ ☾

beside you
is where i find my place
in the universe

i've never loved being me
as much as i do now
being with you

♛ ♦ ♀ ✦ ♥ ❦ ♠ ☾

the cutest thing
is when we walk through a garden
and the bees harmoniously
hover around you
mistaking you for a flower
oh silly bee, oh silly me
i too make the same mistake

when i take you places
i feel like you're a bleeding bella
in a room full of vampires

she didn't want flowers
she didn't want diamonds
all she wanted was poetry
from his heart
to hers

let your life collapse
like a nebula cloud
and just like that
you'll see
a star is born

in order to exist
all things need opposites
yin and yang
hot and cold
him and her

i'll wait and i'll wait
'til life has left me
'til death comes calling
old and grey
because i'm madly in love
hopelessly devoted
to a star that stole my heart

i love the spaces
between our messages
the hour waits
where i am left
in a state of bliss
melting
from the loving words
you left me with

my heart is female
with blonde hair and blue eyes
it walks around outside of my chest
laughing at the strangest things
my heart has a smile too
one for me and one for you
its personality makes me feel adored
keeping me alive through all of my flaws
and did you know
it smells of roses and victoria's secret
bombshell to be precise, it's nice
my little american heart
beating, beating, beating me
back to life

♛ ♦ ♀ ✦ ♥ 🦃 ♠ ☾

falling in love with you
was such a wonderful experience
sometimes i wish we could
fall out of love
just so i could experience
the fall
over and over
again and again

remember that night
i placed my hand on your hip
and lightly called for you
waking you in the night
just to tell you i love you
then half-asleep
you pull my arm
up to your chest, tightly
as if it were a fallen blanket
and whisper ever so gently
"i love you more"

♛ ♦ ♀ ✦ ♥ ☡ ♠ ☾

bees and honey
sugar too
all things sweet
remind me of you

find that special someone
and kiss them
under the moonlight

if your heart swells
you know they're the one

i see you in the morning
staring at your reflection
scanning your face for faults
halt and think to yourself
imperfection, imperfection
and it breaks my heart every single time
i wish i could lend you my eyes
so you could see the masterpiece
that you are

there's something
in the way she loves

it always leaves you
begging for more

i've been classically conditioned
like pavlov's dogs
to smile when i hear the sound
of a message alert
even though it's not always her
i still grin like a cheshire cat
instantaneously

always take care of your lady
treat her like gold
she is the universe
love her
show her
breathe her

just like that
she slew the devil inside her mind
wayward whispers faded
and she stepped forward
into the heavenly light
right where she belongs

thoughts
of you
fall, twirl, drop
like ever so pretty
petals

i used to think
i understood love
like it was something
that could be understood

i wasn't living before i met you
i was just existing, waiting
marking time

she was extraordinarily beautiful
i'll give her that
but it was her soul
that made her special

in the eyes of my lover
i found a thousand reasons
why she earns the title
my lover

once in a blue moon
a kiss catches fire
and leaves you
burning in love

come with me
i'll love you better

she lives a life
of diamonds and pearls
a queen of orange county
still i am just a country boy
and in the soil i find my home

you're tiny like a cupcake
sweet like one too
so tasty and perfect
i
love
you

i've never
had thoughts of forever
until i met you
that in itself tells me
you're the one

our hearts fell in love
and our minds found a way

♛ ♦ ♀ ✦ ♥ 🍄 ♠ ☾

what you don't know about her
is that if she loves you
she'll love every part of you
so much
that you'll start to question
if this is all a dream

they pull a dandelion
making a wish
to never lose the treasure they found
and unbeknown to them
there is an ancient law
old as time
which states you cannot lose
what's true

♛ ♦ ♀ ✦ ♥ 🐮 ♠ ☾

let me play your heart
and you will see
we are a symphony

it's when the lights go out
and i'm exhausted from a happy day
i fall asleep
and just before i do
i feel you
running your fingers through my hair
brushing your knuckles over my cheek
it tells me you love me in the kindest way
you show me what love is
every second of every day

♛ ♦ ♀ ✦ ♥ 🂠 ♠ ☾

in the eyes of every woman
i see a little girl
with a bag of dreams
and a hopeful smile

i was a little bit taller
she was a little bit smarter
we both were a lot a bit
in love

the truth
was in the touch
of their skin
always was
always will be

i'm gonna squeeze your little heart
and colour you in
flushed with love a lover's skin
you can wear it daily kissed by morning dew
a lover's coloured skin from me to you
there'll be hickies on your neck
a diamond in the flesh
fire in your heart and perfection in our mess
then one day i'll frame you
and put you on a wall
my mona lisa masterpiece for you i do it all
and when you feel yourself shading
i'll run to you with crayons
a da vinci to your smile
a pillar for the soul
and when you feel your heart fading
i'll run to you with crayons
an artist for the heart
a gift to god

you're beautiful
from head to toe
inside and outside
i hope you know that

i asked the heavens for a gift
and that was when
i found
you

♛ ♦ ♀ ✦ ♥ 🐨 ♠ ☾

with every moonlit sky
i sleep
a little more in love
and with every sunrise
i wake
a little more alive

i found forever
in you

♛ ♦ ♀ ✦ ♥ 🐁 ♠ ☾

i want to ride with you
along the canals of paris
with a basket full of food
and a bottle of wine
stop off for some
"café et pain au chocolat"
as we eat drink and laugh
without a care in the world
then when we are done
dining on french dishes
we can sit by the eiffel
for a kiss full of wishes

when the time comes
don't say no
because of how you think
my feelings could change
say yes because you know
yours won't

i want
to grow you a garden of uncut flowers
and fill the spaces with your dreams
i want you to wake up every morning
to love heart coffee and a kiss from yours truly
with the sun highlighting your perfect body
i want you to sit in the garden i have grown
and watch you smile at me
as i tell you all the reasons
you are too good
for this world

moonlight and her
go together like
bees and honey

she was
a wild rose
and i was in love
with every
petal

i know where to look
if i ever need to find you
you'll be up there
lying on the tops of clouds
waiting for me

playing with her hair
was a therapy
that healed
my deepest scars

the more time i spend with you
the more i start believing
in miracles

i'd love to welcome you to my world
introduce you to all its residents
but if you ever left i would be embarrassed
for them to know of the treasure
i once held and lost

there's something holy
about loving someone
exactly as they are
it almost feels
as if it's precisely
what god wants

the world seemed to smile
with every breath
she took

it was a love story
from day one

♛ ♦ ♀ ✦ ♥ ☙ ♠ ☾

when you see a girl
for who she is
and you begin to realise
that words will never describe
the infinite perfection
that is her

you know she's the one
when she helps you
love the parts of you
that you never could

his love for her grew feet
and walked a thousand miles
his love for her grew wings
and flew five thousand more
his love for her gained courage
becoming fearless in the eyes of many
his love for her evolved
so new, so new

i wish we could skip to chapter 19
you know the part with you
walking down an aisle to me

♛ ♦ ♀ ◆ ♥ ☙ ♠ ☾

when the last butterfly falls
and the last river runs
we'll still be together
in another place
another land
that's the magic
of love

i'd never imagined a kiss
could empty my mind
and fill my soul
so perfectly

love is a deadly trade
that offers bliss
and bitterness
simultaneously

i know you love the beauty of life
inside yourself and the world
because you are an angel
that likes to see life flourish and not perish
when your eyes see decay
when you see things fall away
it hurts your heart a little
so take these flowers
uncut just how you like them
and know i left them in the ground
just to see you smile

he made a world
of silk and stars
then placed her
in the centre

i want to lie in a soft bed
with my beautiful wife
reciting stories of our beautiful life
just two lovers in the wild night

find someone
you can love with all your heart
you can climb
the highest mountain for
and in return
they will only love you more

she let me love her
and she was easy to love
because don't we all
love perfect things

bliss is born winding through her hair
dreams are made from her luscious lips
her body is a temple of roses and crocus
from her sun-kissed skin the honey drips
drawing me in as if i were a bee
my mind empties then blooms
thoughts of her flirtatiously flower
while the sun shines heaven
come high noon

i look forward to a future
filled with unconditional love
i look forward to making memories
and sharing each other
but out of all the new
amazing things we will do
i'm most excited to lie down
after a day of fun
and cuddle to warm our hearts

♛ ♦ ♀ ✦ ♥ ☕ ♠ ☾

i promise you
this will not be
your destruction
this will be your birth

she was always
the most beautiful in the room
and i was always
the luckiest

we were a mess
in each other's love

nothing in this world
breaks like a heart
and nothing in this world
loves more

i adore date nights
i like walks along the beach
but nothing compares
to being at home with you
in our own little world
making memories
out of simple love

she wore my heart like a crown
and i called her
majesty

♛ ♦ ♀ ✦ ♥ 🜨 ♠ ☾

did i love her first
then fall in love
with all her quirks and traits
or did i love
all her quirks and traits
then fall in love with her

there will come a time
when i will ask of you
something no man should
unless he knows the depth of love
inside his mind, heart and soul

they swapped hearts
and risked it all
just for a chance
at true love

♛ ♦ ♀ ✦ ♥ 🌹 ♠ ☾

i thought i needed god
to find peace
but your kiss has gifted me
tranquility

you'll forever be
my first thought when i wake
and my last thought before i sleep
so please don't ever think
even if it's just for one second
that you aren't always here
with me

we were drunk on love
and the world was ours
one moment at a time
under distant stars

there will always be that moment
of when we first laid eyes
on the person
we now call home

rainy days like these
are for movies, tea and biscuits
then you wrap her in a blanket
and kiss those perfect lips

an hourglass figure
yet when i gaze upon her
time is so absent

"he lights my heart" she said
"i want for nothing in life
but his smile and his love
with the occasional dandelion
placed on our table"

i just want you all to know
she tastes like
peaches and cream

a kiss on the lips
a cup of tea
and a sweet "good morning"
is how everyone
should be starting
their day

spend an hour with her
and she'll have you believing
in fairy tale magic
because that's
the kind of princess
she is

how fast can you fall in love?
a second, a minute
an hour, a day?
maybe even an instant

she was wild at heart
caged from the start
and i wanted nothing more
than to set her free

i loved rainy days
because the rain was my excuse
to curl up on the sofa
with tea, blankets and her
i would play with her beautiful blonde hair
calmed by its velvet feel
and she would snuggle into my arm
sanctified by our skin touching
moments like these are what life is all about
two creatures in a natural habitat
in love with the company they share
and madly in love
with each other's soul

just focus on loving me
and i'll do the rest

she sometimes wondered
if snowflakes
were actually kisses
from heaven

tell her she's beautiful
not to remind her
but simply because
it's true

in the presence of perfection
time evaporates
fractional distillation
at its best

we threw paper planes
with paper tales
of how our love
would last
a lifetime

that night in paris
when the stars aligned for us
our immortal kiss

♛ ♦ ♀ ✦ ♥ ꙮ ♠ ☾

they all fall in love
with some part of her
be it brains, beauty
or her enchanting aura
either way they all fall
one by one
surrendered

👑 ♦ ♀ ✦ ♥ 🐚 ♠ ☾

do you believe it's possible
that somehow
i've wished you into existence?

i only ask this
because for years, every night
when my head would touch a pillow
i'd close my eyes and dream
of finding a love like you

♔ ♦ ♀ ✦ ♥ 🙶 ♠ ☾

we sat on the moon
sipping on starlight
drunk on freedom
we fell

i don't know how it happened
all i know
is that we have filled each other's
broken pieces
with parts of ourselves
and it was in that moment
two became one

one forbidden tropical kiss
closing eyes to make a wish
stars are born on lover's lips
riding a train to truro city

it wasn't just her love
it was the way she loved
like somehow her heart
was always destined
to be mine

lie down my darling angel
and rest your wings
tonight

♛ ♦ ♀ ✦ ♥ ☙ ♠ ☾

her lips are the doorway
to that place
you've always dreamed of

♛ ♦ ♀ ✦ ♥ 🥀 ♠ ☾

she was classy
with a dash of mess

since the day we met
i've had this vision of me and you
walking through the snow
hand in hand holding a rose
i'd smile at my baby blonde
for seeing you so happy
like a little winter girl
making snow angels
on the tundra
of tomorrow

♛ ♦ ♀ ✦ ♥ ♉ ♠ ☾

i don't know the stars very well
but i love them enough
to know i want them in the sky
forever

sometimes
the greatest gift
is letting someone
love you

hearts beat to the sound of breath
while senses peak and necks drip sweat
in that moment of collision
honey-soaked passion
they find truth in the touch
of their skin

she took away
the emptiness inside

tell me you love me
once a day
and my heart
will be yours
forever

in the face of my lover
i found stars
in the face of my lover
i found freedom
in the face of my lover
i found god galore
i guess you could say
she is the universe

love her like royalty

like a crow knows its way
around the night sky
i know my way around you
your body is a maze
i have traced delicately
inch by inch
leaving you
complete

from the moment
i laid eyes on her i knew
that my life would be spent
changing our stars
so we could be aligned
in this life and the next

you fill the lacuna
in my heart

somebody
fell in love with me
and i wonder how
every day

have you ever looked
at the heart and soul
of the one you love
and questioned how the universe
made something so beautiful
out of nothing?

i never knew
that i could feel like a bird in the sky
i never knew
the love from you could make me feel so high
and now i'm ready
just to stay with you and trickle through time
and now i'm ready
just to hold you 'til the end of my life

so i want you to stay
i want you to know
i'm ready to go wherever you go
and i want you to know that you saved me from life
i need you to know everything is all right

you don't need a reason
to love

she wanted to see beauty
beyond her wildest dreams
so he gave her a mirror
and told her to never forget
her divinity

you hide behind flowers as if to say
their beauty outshines your hidden face
silly girl, silly girl
stop being a fool
everyone knows
you are the fairest
of them all

true love can't be killed

i often reminisce
on the early mornings we shared
when i would bring tea to the table
still dazed from a dream
i would sip away gazing
while you applied your makeup
watching you would have this
therapeutic effect on me
everything was so dreamy, still, quiet
the sun would shine
giving your face a holy glow
it's in those moments of beauty
that i would know
i would know you are the one for me
and always will be
i would know the time we have
will never be enough
i would know that you are truly special
and that those simple moments with you
are what i will cherish
for the rest of our life

♛ ♦ ♀ ✦ ♥ ☕ ♠ ☾

you'll never believe
how perfect you look
when you're asleep
caught in a dream

sometimes i lie on my bed
hands behind my head
and i think about you
i think about
the amazing person you are
and how lucky i am to have you
i get lost in hues in happiness
i get lost in your sweetness
you are my saviour
my valentine
my angel

i've found poetry in the locks of her hair
i've seen poetry in the depth of her eyes
i've touched poetry on the surface of her skin
she is and always will be
the greatest poem i'll ever read

all i can taste is your sweetness
all i can feel is your love
moments with you are forever
memories of you fill me up
no bleeding to make my heart beat
we'll catch each other if we fall
this love can never be broken
together we have the world
and i know that the world will judge us
they'll stare in confusion alone
but in that moment i'll pity their souls
for what we have they'll never know
now i don't need the world to save me
because baby you already have
and i don't need a life of lavish
you're heaven in the palm of my hand

i like your soul
i just like it
maybe i'm obsessed

♛ ♦ ♀ ✦ ♥ 🐱 ♠ ☾

a sunset
a beach
and a bottle of wine
is all that was needed
to ignite the love
inside their hearts

she loves me
she knows me
her cold touch warms me
her wildly wakeful whispers
are like music to my ears
a match made in black
twin hearts coagulate
unbreakable bonds form
and the tower of truth crumbles
blood magic, rituals of love
we dance around the fire
with diamonds in our hands
a wedding of two worlds
and a guest list of boundaries

time, space and love
i invite you all

♛ ♦ ♀ ✦ ♥ 🦗 ♠ ☾

will you be
my never-ending fairy tale
as i kiss you silly

ouch!
cupid shot me

♛ ♦ ♀ ✦ ♥ 🐣 ♠ ☾

they were stargazing lovers
upon the hills of tomorrow
wishing that their hearts
would stay forever twisted

we woke to a cornish morning
looking out to the castle on the mount
i knew that today was the day
i was going to give you that diamond ring
down on one knee
a queen, a castle
and her soon to be king

sometimes
i go to bed early
with a scent of you on my wrist
from the perfume you sent me
and a memory of your kiss
i do this on nights
when i miss you a little more
i adore you so much
i adore, i adore

♛ ♦ ♀ ✦ ♥ 🐛 ♠ ☾

snowflakes shimmer
through the echo of time
and kiss this broken face
rejuvenated, alive
we breathe once more
through fire and ice we fall
and through us
we rise

in all her splendour
i lost my heart
serenity spilt
and i fell deep
into unknown territory

i'm just crazy in love with you
it's as simple as that

she is a star
the brightest star you'll ever see
and i'm going to marry her
and make her happy
for eternity

know that one day we'll be close
with wedding rings and a sunny home
no more kisses through a broken phone
just me and you
no more alone

promise yourself
that you'll never give up hope in finding love
promise yourself
that if you lose it you'll find it again
promise yourself
that you'll keep on searching
because the pursuit of love
is and always will be
one of the purest forms of living
so i ask the lost souls
to put your wavering thoughts to bed
and instead
live to love
so that one day soon
you'll love to live
every minute of every day
in love

THANK YOU

Dear Readers,

I want to take this moment to thank all of the fans who have supported me since I began writing and all of the new readers who have just discovered this book. I want you all to know that your messages of love and appreciation have touched me. I'll always be eternally grateful. Keep spreading love to the people who come and go in your life and try to leave them better than they were before. Love is simple, love is life, may you all find an everlasting love that makes you feel alive.

Take care, I love you all x

- Kira

ABOUT THE AUTHOR

Kira was raised in Cornwall, England.
He started writing poems on instagram and
quickly found a devoted audience of thousands
worldwide who connect with his timeless romantic
poetry. The lens he sees love through is innocent
yet absolute. Hearts rise up to meet his words.

♛ ♦ ♀ ✦ ♥ ♔ ♠ ☾

Printed in Great Britain
by Amazon

61465957R00104